T0071140

Reena Esmail

SHE WILL TRANSFORM YOU

SECULAR | SSATB | ORCHESTRA

VOCAL SCORE

OXFORD
UNIVERSITY PRESS

OXFORD
UNIVERSITY PRESS

Great Clarendon Street, Oxford OX2 6DP,
United Kingdom

Oxford University Press is a department of the University of Oxford.
It furthers the University's objective of excellence in research, scholarship,
and education by publishing worldwide. Oxford is a registered trade mark of
Oxford University Press in the UK and in certain other countries

© Oxford University Press 2023

Reena Esmail has asserted her right under the Copyright, Designs
and Patents Act, 1988, to be identified as the Composer of this Work

First published 2023

Impression: 1

All rights reserved. No part of this publication may be reproduced,
stored in a retrieval system, or transmitted, in any form or by any means,
without the prior permission in writing of Oxford University Press

Permission to perform this work in public (except in the course of divine worship)
should normally be obtained from a local performing right licensing organization,
unless the owner or the occupier of the premises being used already holds
a licence from such an organization. Likewise, permission to make and
exploit a recording of this work should be obtained from a
local mechanical copyright licensing organization

Enquiries concerning reproduction outside the scope of the above
should be directed to the Music Rights Department, Oxford University Press,
at music.permissions.uk@oup.com or at the address above

ISBN 978–0–19–356488–6

Music and text origination by Katie Johnston

Printed in Great Britain on acid-free paper by
Halstan & Co. Ltd, Amersham, Bucks.

Composer's note

She Will Transform You explores the idea of belonging and is centred around a powerful poem by Indian-American author Neelanjana Banerjee. Told through the voice of an immigrant mother, who feels shunned by both her country of origin and her country of residence, this piece is a fervent prayer for her child: that, with a little bit of kindness from the child's environment, they might have the power and perspective to embrace and connect both cultures.

As a child of immigrants myself, I have felt that distance—of being the 'other' in both America and India—and also the resonance of being at home in either place.

The piece moves in and out of a Hindustani raga called Rageshree, which has such a lush resonance; it is also harmonically grounded in an unusual way, containing no 5th scale degree, which makes our ear feel like it's never quite 'home'. As a result, it has both a sense of belonging and one of distance. It is these two feelings, and the journey between them, that I wanted to explore in this work.

This note may be reproduced as required for programme notes.

Duration: 16 minutes

Instrumentation

2 flutes (2nd doubling piccolo)
2 oboes
2 clarinets in B♭
2 bassoons
4 horns in F
2 trumpets in B♭
3 trombones
tuba
timpani
percussion—2 or 3 players (suspended cymbal, glockenspiel, vibraphone)
harp
celeste
strings

Full scores and instrumental parts are available on hire/rental.

This piece is also available in an independent version for SSATB and flute (ISBN 978–0–19–356480–0).

Commissioned by the University of Richmond Department of Music
for the 2018–2019 Tucker-Boatwright Festival of Literature and the Arts

She Will Transform You

Neelanjana Banerjee (b. 1978), altd

REENA ESMAIL

© Oxford University Press 2023

Printed in Great Britain

OXFORD UNIVERSITY PRESS, MUSIC DEPARTMENT, GREAT CLARENDON STREET, OXFORD OX2 6DP

The Moral Rights of the Composer have been asserted. Photocopying this copyright material is ILLEGAL.

* Fanned beams indicate a gradual speeding up through the beamed group.

B
27
p
mf
p
30
f
p
C
Serene
35
mp
f
mf
p
f
39
mp
42
mf
mp
RH
mf
p

45
mf
mp
mf
RH
mf
p
48
Press ahead ♩ = c.60
3
mp
RH
D Serene ♩ = c.44
52
1
2
mp
E - lude me,
A.
mp
3
Home-land, why do you e - lude me, e - lude me,
T.
mp
3
p (stagger breathing)
Home-land, why do you e-lude me? mm
B.
mp
p (stagger breathing)
Home - land, why, mm
D Serene ♩ = c.44
3
3

57
mp
E - lude me, tease me,
tease me, e - lude me, tease me,
tease me, e - lude me, tease me, e -
60
p
e - lude me?
e - lude me, e - lude me, e - lude me?
- lude me, e - lude me, e - lude me?

E Press ahead ♩ = c.60
63
S.
A.
T.
B.
mp
mf
There, my an - ces - tors don't know me.
Here, my neigh-bors say
E Press ahead ♩ = c.60
66
'go back home, back home, back
'go back home' to me, 'back home' to me, 'back
'go back home' to me, 'back home' to me, 'back
back'.
'go back home, back home, back
rit.
p

69
Serene ♩ = c.44
S. 1
home'.
When will you let me
S. 2
home'.
When will you let me
A.
home'. Home - land, when will you let me name you,
T.
home'. Home - land, when will you let me name you,
Home - land,
B.
home'. Home - land, home - land,
Serene ♩ = c.44
72
name you, let me claim you,
name you, let me claim you,
let me claim you,
name you, claim, claim you, let me
name you, claim you,

76
F
mp
p
name you,
name you,
name you,
name you,
name you,
name you,
let me
name you,
F
79
claim you,
name
claim you,
name you,
claim you,
name you,
claim you,
let me name you,
name you,
claim you,
name you,

83
you,
claim you?
claim you?
claim you?
claim you?
claim you?
Più mosso ♩ = c.52
86
89
92

rit.
G Flowing ♩ = c.80
97
mp
S.
But now, it is no long - er, long -
A.
But now, it is no long - er, long -
T.
But now, long - er,
B.
But now, long - er,
rit.
G Flowing ♩ = c.80
mp
101
- er a - bout me, no long - er,
- er a - bout me, no long - er,
long - er, no long - er a - bout
me, no long - er,

105
for this new - born child, new - born child I have a
for this new - born child, new - born child I have a
me— for this new, for this new-born child, new-born child I have a
— for this new - born child, new - born child,
110
plea, a plea, a plea:
plea, a plea, a plea, a plea, a plea:
plea, a plea, a plea, a plea, a plea:
a plea, a plea, a plea, a plea:
plea, plea:
p
mf
p
f

H
115
f
Home, home - land, sweet child be,
Home, home - land, let this sweet, sweet child be,
Home - land, let this sweet child, child be,
Home, home - land, let this sweet child be,
H
120
ne-ver tor - ture her like you've done to
ne-ver tor - ture her like you've done, you've done to
ne-ver tor - ture, tor - ture her like you've done to
ne-ver tor - ture her like you've done to

125
me. Let her find
me, to me. Let her al - ways find her,
me, to me. Let her al - ways find
me. Let her al - ways
129
her way, her way—
find her way—
mp poco a poco cresc.
sur-face streets and
her way—
mp poco a poco cresc.
sur-face streets
find her way—
mp poco a poco cresc.
sur - face streets,
I
I
mp poco a poco cresc.

133
mp poco a poco cresc.
and high - ways, un-der-pass-es and bike - paths,
high - ways, sur-face streets. and high - ways, and
and high-ways, un-der-pass-es and bike-paths,
high - ways, sur - face streets, high - ways,
136
f
and high - ways, and high - ways. She will trans - form you,
sur-face streets and high-ways, and high - ways. She will trans - form you,
un-der-pass-es and bike-paths. She will trans - form you,
sur - face streets, high - ways. She will trans - form you,
mf

140
mp
trans-form you
mp
trans-form you
mf
she will trans-form you
mp
trans-form you,
p
f
146
J
mp
from con-cept
mp
from con-cept to com - mu-ni - ty, from skid row to
mp
from con-cept to com-mu-ni - ty, from con-cept
mp
con - cept, com - mu - ni - ty, con - cept, com-
J
mp

150
to com-mu-ni-ty, from con-cept, to safe ha-ven,
safe ha-ven, to safe ha-ven, to safe ha-ven, to
to com-mu-ni-ty, from con-cept to com-mu-ni-ty,
-mu-ni-ty, com-mu-ni-ty, com-mu-ni-ty, com-
153
to safe ha-ven, she will trans-form you, trans-form you,
safe ha-ven, she will trans-form you, trans-form you,
to com-mu-ni-ty, she will trans-form, trans-form you,
-mu-ni-ty, she will trans-form you, trans-form
p
mp

158
p
mf
she will trans - form you.
she will trans - form you.
she will trans - form, trans - form you. With each mile - stone,
f
you, trans - form you. With each mile - stone,
163
K
Let her dis-man-tle your dis-tance, un-til one day,
Let her dis - man - tle your dis - tance, your dis-tance, un-til one day,
let her dis - man - tle your dis - tance, un-til one day,
let her dis - man - tle your dis - tance, un-til one day,

168
she ar - rives here—
palm tree
she ar - rives here—
palm tree sha - dow, des - ert
she ar - rives— palm tree sha - dow, des - ert dust in her eyes, dust
(stagger breathing)
she ar - rives here, mm
(stagger breathing)
she ar - rives here, mm
173
sha - dow, des - ert dust in her eyes, dust in her eyes, dust
dust in her eyes, dust in her eyes,
in her eyes, dust in her eyes, dust in her eyes, dust in her
LH

177
pp
in her eyes—
p
and
dust in her eyes—
and
eyes, dust in her eyes—
(mm)
(mm)
181
L Serene ♩ = c.44
smiles, and knows, she's home.
smiles, and knows, she's home.
and smiles, and knows.
Home-land,
and smiles, and knows.
Home-land,
and smiles, and knows.
Home-land,
L Serene ♩ = c.44

186
mp
She will trans-form you,
p
She will trans-form you,
mp
trans - form you,
mp
she will trans - form you, trans -
p
she will trans - form you,
p (stagger breathing)
mm
(stagger breathing)
home - land,
home - land,
mm
mp

190
mp
trans - form you, trans-form you,
trans - form you, trans - form you, trans-form you,
- form you, trans - form you, trans-form you, trans-

193
she will trans - form you, trans -
trans - form you, trans - form you, trans - form you,
- form you, trans - form you, trans - form you,
(mm) home - land,
(mm) home - land,
196
- form you, trans - form you.
trans - form you.
trans-form you, trans-form you, trans-form you.
home - land, home - land.
home - land, home - land.
niente